# MADE IN THE RENAISSANCE

Arts and Crafts of the
Age of Exploration

Written and Illustrated by
CHRISTINE PRICE

E. P. DUTTON & COMPANY, INC., NEW YORK

FOR MY FATHER
who showed me the New World

Contents

FOREWORD

THE EXAMPLES OF THE ARTS AND CRAFTS OF THE
Renaissance, pictured in this book, come from
museums and libraries in England and the United
States. My grateful thanks are due to the Trustees
of the British Museum; the Metropolitan Museum
of Art; the Museum of Fine Arts, Boston; the New
York Historical Society; the Victoria and Albert
Museum; the Yale School of Music and the Yale
University Art Gallery for their courtesy in per-
mitting me to include examples from their col-
lections.

I am also grateful to Mr. Henry C. Taylor for
permission to use the illustrations on Pages 110,
115 and 116, from books in his collection; to the

8

Boston Public Library for the woodcut on Page 118; and to the Yale University Library for the book illustrations on Pages 13, 85, 104, 107 and 117, and for the playing cards on Pages 93 and 98.

The illustrations on Pages 109, 111, 112, 113 and 119 are taken from *Decorative Printed Maps of the 15th to 18th Centuries* by R. A. Skelton (The Staples Press, London, 1952) and are included here by kind permission of the publishers.

The illustration of the printing press on Page 100 and the printer's mark on Page 104 come from *The Book* by Henri Bouchot (Scribner and Welford, New York, 1890).

I would also like to thank everyone who has helped me in the making of this book. I am especially grateful to Miss Elizabeth Chase of the Yale University Art Gallery, who read the manuscript and made valuable criticisms and suggestions.

In these pages I have been able to show only a handful of the beautiful things that were made in the Renaissance. I hope that the list of museums at the end of the book, telling specifically where each object may be found, will be an invitation to some readers to go out and see the things that are pictured here and to discover many more of the wonderful works of Renaissance craftsmen.

C. P.

9

The Craftsmen and Their World

THE RENAISSANCE HAS OFTEN BEEN called the Age of Exploration. This was the time of Columbus and the discovery of America; of Vasco da Gama, who found the sea route to India; and of Magellan, who set out to sail around the globe.

Year after year, in the fifteenth and sixteenth centuries, the explorers ventured farther from the world they knew. They sailed southward down the coast of Africa and passed boldly through the Torrid Zone, where the sea was said to be boiling hot; and they braved the storms of the open Atlantic, once thought of as the Sea of Darkness leading to

10

the edge of the world. Whether they sailed to the south, to the west, or to the ice-choked seas of the north, the goal of the first explorers was the same. They were searching for a new way to the fabulous lands of the East, to the silks and jewels and the palaces paved with gold, and, above all, to the mysterious islands where the spices grew.

Cloves, cinnamon and allspice, nutmeg, ginger and pepper ranked with the greatest treasures of the East. Spices were necessities for all who could afford to buy them. They added varied and exciting flavors to food and drink; and in the cold hungry winters, when pigs and cattle were slaughtered and people lived largely on smoked and salted meat, spices were used for preserving the meat as well as improving its taste.

In the Middle Ages spices had been brought to Europe by camel caravans across Asia, or up the Red Sea to Alexandria in Egypt; but the source of the spices remained a mystery, even to the merchants of Venice whose wealth was founded on Eastern trade. It was not until the beginning of the sixteenth century that Portuguese explorers first sighted the Spice Islands of the Pacific, where nutmeg and cloves grew on evergreen trees.

While the Portuguese were bringing home cargoes of silks and spices by the sea route of Vasco

11

COVERED CUP IN THE
SHAPE OF A GLOBE

da Gama, the Spaniards were exploring the New World. Armored conquistadors raided the glittering treasuries of the Incas and Aztecs. They battled their way across the continent, through deserts and tropical forests and over icy mountains; and Spanish ships launched out into the vast Pacific Ocean, in the wake of Magellan, to seize a share of the trade with the East.

The sea captains and explorers could never have made their great journeys without the help of the people they left behind. Princes and rich merchants gave money to fit out fleets of ships. Scientists provided the explorers with maps and globes and instruments of navigation. Shipwrights and blacksmiths and makers of ropes and sails built new ships and refitted old ones to sail the unknown seas. Finally there were the craftsmen who made all the other things necessary to equip an expedition — the makers of clothes and armor and weapons, the coopers who made casks for storing food and water, the makers of pots and pans for cooking, the glassworkers who supplied colored beads for trade goods, and the goldsmiths who made silver cups and plates for the captain's cabin.

These craftsmen of the Renaissance worked by hand as their forefathers had done in the Middle Ages. In the towns where most of them lived, the

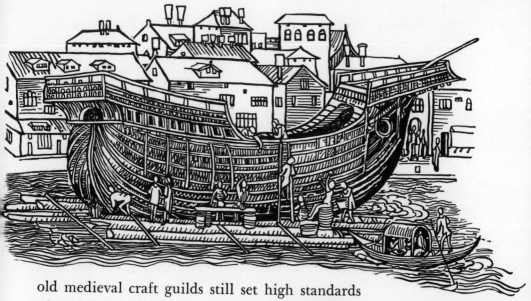

old medieval craft guilds still set high standards
of workmanship. Craftsmen had to undergo a long
training as apprentices and journeymen before
they could be masters and open shops of their own.

The streets of towns were lined with the small
shops of the craftsmen. In one street, there were
tailors stitching clothes; nearby were shoemakers
or hatters or a row of goldsmiths' shops with a
glittering show of jewelry. Another street echoed
to the clang of the armorer's hammer, and in another, craftsmen were at work on carvings and embroideries for the Church. Shops like these had
been familiar sights during the Middle Ages, but
in the fifteenth century a new craft was born, and

SHIPBUILDING IN VENICE
*Detail from an illustration
in Bernhard Breidenbach's
Journey to the Holy Land
Mainz, 1486*

PRINTING SHOP
*from an engraving
by Theodor Galle
Dutch, 1570-1633*

a new kind of shop was opened in the towns and cities of Europe. Printed books were displayed on the counter, and in the workroom a master printer directed his journeymen as they set type, printed the pages on a press, and hung them up to dry, ready to be bound into books.

In the Middle Ages all books were copied out by hand. They were few and expensive and mostly written in Latin, the language of scholars. With the invention of printing in the Renaissance, books could be published in hundreds and thousands, and many of them were written in German, French, Italian, and other languages of the people. Customers at a bookshop browsed among religious

14

works, books of poetry, plays and stories, and thrilling accounts of the voyages of the explorers; but to many readers the most important books of all were the new editions of the literature of ancient Greece and Rome.

The writings of Roman authors were preserved in medieval manuscripts; but the work of the Greeks had been newly discovered by Italian scholars and opened to readers a whole world of fresh, exciting ideas. In the Middle Ages the Church had taught people to be humble before the power of God and to think more about Heaven than about the earth on which they lived. The Greeks, on the other hand, had boundless curiosity about the natural world around them, and they believed that men were not lowly sinners but god-like beings with the power to do great things. In the Renaissance the works of the Greek thinkers, poets, and scientists were not only read by scholars; they were quickly translated from Greek into Latin, and even into the languages of the people so that many might read them. Explorers studied the maps and writings of Ptolemy, the great geographer of Alexandria; and noblemen, in their splendid palaces, discussed the philosophy of Plato.

The Italian princes of the Renaissance were famous patrons of art and learning, employing

15

PRINTER'S MARK
OF ALDUS MANUTIUS

scores of artists and craftsmen to decorate their palaces and to design pageants, processions, and magnificent entertainments. Princes and nobles of other lands vied with the Italians in splendor and summoned Italian craftsmen to their courts, bringing new ideas and new styles of art.

France, England, and Spain had strong rulers in the sixteenth century, and old ways of life and thought were changing. The medieval system of powerful feudal lords was breaking down, and people were beginning to think of themselves not as followers of their lord, but as citizens of their country and subjects of their king. They even questioned the beliefs of the Church which had united men for so long, and religious reformers rose up to lead a great revolt against the Church's power. The Reformation of the sixteenth century brought terrible religious wars and persecutions, and men and women on both sides fought and died for what they believed to be true.

Artists and craftsmen of the Renaissance were used to war and violence, whether they worked at the courts of kings or in their own shops. Sometimes they had to be quick with sword and dagger and fight for their lives. Yet they still delighted in fine workmanship, in the delicate setting of a jewel in a ring, the pattern of an embroidered

EMBROIDERED FIGURE
OF A FALCONER

16

glove, or the chiseled carving of a sword hilt.

When we speak of the art of the Renaissance, we usually think first of the great painters and sculptors, whom we set apart from craftsmen as workers in the "fine arts." But it is chiefly the work of the craftsmen, in wood and clay, metal and gems, cloth and paper, that we shall see in this book. In the Renaissance there was no rigid division between arts and crafts. Painters and sculptors, though highly respected, belonged to craft guilds like other workers, and they were often masters of many skills. Sculptors might turn to designing jewelry or armor, while painters used their art in the decoration of furniture and pottery.

The Renaissance is a difficult time to confine between dates, for it was not a tidy historical period with a beginning and an end. The things we shall look at were made between 1450, just before the birth of Columbus, and 1650, after the first colonists had settled in the New World.

The word Renaissance means "rebirth" and refers to the revival of the classical art and learning of Greece and Rome. It also means the rebirth of the spirit of adventure that drove men out to explore far lands and seas and made the Renaissance such an exciting time to live in, like a spring morning, fresh and new and full of hope.

17

MARINER'S COMPASS

AND DIVIDERS

Clothes and Textiles

LOTHES WERE MAGNIFICENT IN THE
Renaissance. People paraded like
peacocks in silks, velvets, and bro-
cades, and princes displayed their
wealth and power by the richness of
their dress. When Henry VIII of England sailed to
France in 1520 to meet the French king, Francis I,
their meeting near Calais was the occasion of a
mighty contest in splendor, remembered ever afterward as the Field of the Cloth of Gold. The followers of the two kings spent whole fortunes on
dress. Some must have worn suits of Italian satin
as beautiful as this red damask with its design of
golden animals. Others were resplendent in velvet,

Above,
ITALIAN COSTUME
About 1505
Opposite,
ENGLISH COSTUME
1520-1530

18

FANCY SATIN
OR DAMASK
Italian,
16th century

FLEMISH COSTUME
Detail from a
Flemish tapestry,
early 16th century

brocaded with threads of precious metal, like the
Italian velvet opposite, boldly patterned in crim-
son and silver.

Italy was the leader of fashion, and the wonder-

ful materials made by Italian silk weavers were eagerly sought after in northern Europe. Merchants of Antwerp, in Flanders, stocked their shops with silks and velvets from Venice and Florence, Bologna, Milan, and Naples; and from Antwerp to Italy, in return, went bales of the famous Flemish woolens — hard-wearing cloth for the clothes of country folk, and soft, supple fabrics as luxurious as velvet.

The man and woman on the left are dressed in the ample, fur-trimmed clothes of wealthy citizens of Flanders in the early 1500's. The man wears square-toed shoes in the German fashion,

21

PEASANT COSTUME
German, 16th century

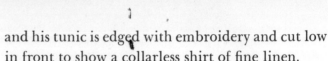

RETICELLO LACE
French or Italian,
late 16th century

and his tunic is edged with embroidery and cut low in front to show a collarless shirt of fine linen.

This loose and easy style of dress did not last for long. Clothes began to grow stiffer and tighter, and in the mid-sixteenth century Europe was swept by the uncomfortable fashion for wearing starched linen ruffs. This was an Italian idea, and the art of making lace, so necessary for the decoration of ruffs, was also born in Italy.

The earliest laces were worked with needle and thread and called "needlepoint." The stiff little figures on the lace at the left were formed by weaving the thread in and out of a piece of fine white netting, while the *reticello* lace was made on a background of linen, cut in an openwork pattern. As their skill increased, the laceworkers dispensed with the foundation of netting or linen and made laces as delicate in design as spiders' webs and known as "point-in-air." Venice was the great center for needlepoint, and with the big demand for lace, the art spread to France, Germany,

NETWORK
Italian, 16th century

MAN'S DOUBLET
*French or Spanish,
late 16th century*

MAN WEARING A RUFF

and Spain. Brussels, in Belgium, became famous for bobbin lace which was made by twisting together a number of separate threads, each one wound on a little bone spindle, or bobbin. The Brussels lacemakers used threads of linen; the Spaniards preferred silk, silver, and gold. This black velvet doublet is trimmed with silver lace and tailored in the close-fitting Spanish style fashionable in the late sixteenth century. It was worn with tight sleeves, long hose, and immensely padded breeches, all of rich material and often covered with embroidery.

23

BOY'S COSTUME
late 16th century

EMBROIDERER AT WORK

BACK OF A CHASUBLE
*Italian, probably
16th century*

PRIEST WEARING
A CHASUBLE

The sixteenth century was a wonderful time for embroidered clothes. Beautiful vestments were made for the Church, like this red velvet chasuble with an embroidered picture of the Crucifixion; but with the coming of the Reformation there was less demand for religious needlework. Services in reformed churches were made simple and plain. Elaborate vestments were swept away, and in Eng-

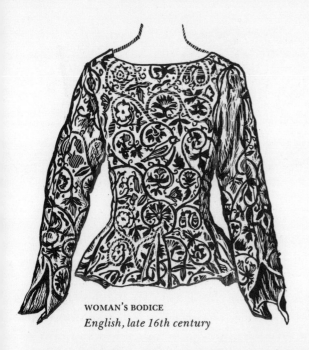

WOMAN'S BODICE
English, late 16th century

DETAIL FROM AN
EMBROIDERY DESIGN
English, early 17th century

land especially, the embroiderers turned to the decoration of dress.

Much of the work was done by noblewomen with plenty of time on their hands, and even queens enjoyed embroidery. Queen Elizabeth I was well-known for her skill with the needle; and, in her collection of more than two thousand gowns, she had many with rich embroidery. One of them, of white satin, was decorated for her by the Countess of Shrewsbury as a Christmas present. In style it was like the dress at the right, the wide stiff skirt padded with a roll of material called a farthingale;

GIRL'S COSTUME
late 16th century

Right, MAN'S CAP
*English, late 16th
or early 17th century*

Below, GLOVE WITH
EMBROIDERED GAUNTLET
*English, early
17th century*

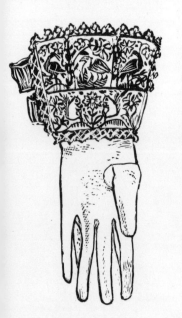

and it was embroidered with birds, fishes, lizards, snakes, spouting whales, and exotic plants — wonders that Elizabeth's sea captains must often have seen on their voyages to the New World.

Embroideries might also glorify the deeds of the wearer. A portrait of Sir Francis Drake, most famous of Elizabethan seamen, shows him with little worlds embroidered all over his doublet to commemorate his sailing around the globe. Such unusual designs were copied from the pictures in books of science and travel, while simple patterns like the flowers and pomegranates on the man's cap could be found in special pattern books. This small cap, trimmed with gold lace and spangles, was meant for informal wear in the house, for men seldom went bareheaded. Gauntlet gloves with cuffs of elaborate needlework were worn by men and women alike. They were sometimes scented with jasmine, and made elegant New Year's gifts.

Above, STAG *from an
embroidered sampler
English, 17th century*

The slashed costume of white satin shows an even more popular way of decorating clothes. The doublet and breeches are cut, or slashed, in little slits to show a different material underneath. This idea is supposed to have originated with the Swiss soldiers who defeated Charles the Bold, Duke of Burgundy, in 1477. When the victors plundered the Duke's camp, they tore his silken tent into strips to mend their ragged clothes, and everyone was so impressed with the effect that it started a new fashion!

27

GERMAN MUSKETEER
IN SLASHED CLOTHES
*from a 16th century
woodcut*

Slashings were also said to represent wounds, signs of a man's bravery in battle, but the fashion soon spread to women's clothes too. Doublets and bodices, sleeves, stockings, breeches, and gloves — all were slashed. There were even slashed shoes, as you can see on page 20. Shoes, like clothes, grew tighter and narrower until both men and women were tottering about on high red heels, and had to protect their shoes by wearing pattens to lift their feet above the dust and mud. Poorer people wore the stout practical footwear which the craftsmen are making and selling in the shoeshop.

28

WOMAN'S LEATHER SHOE
Spanish, 16th century

Below, 17TH CENTURY
COSTUME *Detail from
an engraving by
Abraham Bosse
French, 1637*

During the seventeenth century, slashed and padded clothes gradually gave way to more graceful styles which we can see in this picture of an elegant Parisian couple. Lace, more important than ever, is even used to trim the legs of the man's breeches, which are also adorned with bunches of ribbon. He wears a slender sword, and from the woman's belt hang a hand mirror and a tiny pendant watch.

The stern Puritans declared that it was a sin to wear such finery, but all around them people still believed in a joyful richness of dress and gaily spent their wealth on brilliant stuffs, exquisite lace, and some of the loveliest jewelry ever made.

Jewelry and Watches

GOLD RING WITH DIAMOND
16th century

OLD AND SILVER AND GEMS WERE MORE
plentiful in the Renaissance than
ever before. For hundreds of years
precious stones had been imported
from Persia, India, and Ceylon. Six-
teenth-century jewelry blazed with gems brought
back by the Spaniards from the New World. Emer-
alds from the mines of Colombia and pearls from
South American shores were worked into beautiful pendants to hang about the necks of lords and
ladies. The Spanish treasure ships were rich prizes
for the English sea captains who harried them in

GOLD RING WITH TURQUOISE
16th century

the Caribbean. All England rejoiced when the sea
dogs came home, laden with loot; and nautical
jewels, like the ship pendant with its crystal hull
and golden rigging, must have been worn with
pride by the Elizabethans.

No one was more fond of jewels than Queen
Elizabeth I. The splendid pendant known as the
Armada Jewel, glittering with enameled gold, diamonds, and rubies, was made after the defeat of
the Spanish Armada in 1588 and presented by the
Queen to one of her Privy Councillors for his faith-
ful service in the war against Spain. On the front
of the pendant is her portrait, so finely modeled in
relief that you can see the rich material of her

31

MERMAID PENDANT
*German or Italian,
late 16th century*

CAP-JEWEL WITH
SAINT GEORGE
AND THE DRAGON
probably German,
16th century

gown and the gems in her hair. The back opens like a locket to show a miniature picture of the Queen by Nicholas Hilliard, her court painter, who was also a goldsmith and may have been the designer and maker of the Armada Jewel.

Many painters and sculptors received their early training in the workshops of goldsmiths. Benvenuto Cellini, the most famous goldsmith of the Renaissance, wrote the story of his life, a tale full of strife and adventure. He tells how young men from Italy, Germany and France flocked to his workshop to serve him as apprentices. Cellini worked in Rome and in his native city of Florence and also at the court of the French king, Francis I. The king delighted in fine jewelry and used to wear a collar of diamonds and pearls, and in his hat, a great diamond adorned with hanging rubies.

Brooches to be worn in the hat had long been popular with men. They were decorated with scenes from classical myths, portraits of famous people, and pictures of saints. A favorite subject was Saint George and the Dragon, which we can see in the enameled brooch at the left.

Rings were the most popular jewelry of all, and the hands of the rich were loaded with rings, almost to the fingertips. People still held to the old belief in the magic powers of gems. The turquoise

RING WITH TOADSTONE
15th or 16th century

32

GOLDSMITH'S WORKSHOP
*from an engraving by
the goldsmith,
Etienne Delaulne
French, 16th century*

ring on page 30 was supposed to protect its wearer against a fall from his horse, while the rare toadstone, set in this curious ring of horn and silver, was highly valued for its power to guard the owner against poisoning. Toadstone, brown and shiny, was said to grow in the heads of large and aged toads, but in reality it was the fossilized tooth of a fish!

Engagement rings were often designed in the shape of clasped hands. This one is known as a "gimmal ring," from the Latin word *geminus*,

33

GOLD GIMMAL RING

AGATE WATCH
German, 1625-1650

CRYSTAL WATCH
French, 1600-1625

SILVER WATCH
French, about 1600

meaning twin, and is made to be split into two. The engaged couple could each wear half of it until their wedding day when the halves were brought together to form a wedding ring with the little golden hands neatly clasped. There were fancy rings of all kinds. One was made to open and reveal a removable compass, and another was set with a tiny watch which struck the hours.

Clocks had been used in the Middle Ages, but watches were a new invention. Some of the earliest ones, oval in shape, were made in 1500 by Peter Hele of Nuremberg, and for years afterward watches were known as "Nuremberg eggs." Their mechanism was the work of locksmiths, but their elaborate cases show us the art of the jeweler.

The watch at the top has an agate case set with rubies around the profile portrait of a young man; the middle one is of clear crystal; and the third, in the traditional egg shape, is of silver, finely engraved. All three are designed as pendants, to hang around the neck or from the belt, but watches could also be worn as dangling earrings or set into the hilts of swords and daggers. Swords with such fancy hilts had become a usual part of a gentleman's dress, and we often find them decorated by goldsmiths with all the delicacy and splendor of jewelry.

Weapons for Sport and War

IN THE STORMY DAYS OF THE RENAIS-
sance, weapons were for practical
use, but they were also works of art.
This sword hilt with its curving
guard was shaped by a German hilt-
maker to protect the hand of the swordsman. A
second craftsman adorned the hilt with small figures in relief, chiseled out of the cold iron, a
method which could produce such fine sculpture
as the little Negro's head below. Lastly a goldsmith
decorated the hilt with damascened work, scratching the delicate pattern into the surface of the
metal and inlaying it with silver and gold.

As sword hilts became more ornate, the blades
grew more slender, supple, and sharply pointed.

35

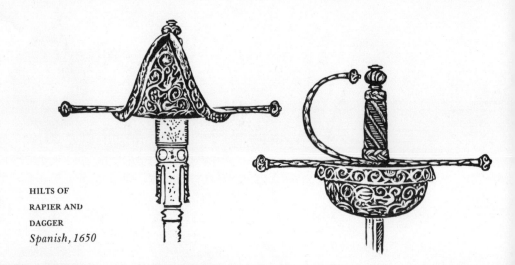

In the sixteenth century the broad-bladed sword of the Middle Ages was replaced, as a weapon for gentlemen, by the needle-sharp rapier; and the mighty two-handed blade, wielded by medieval knights, was taken over by foot soldiers, particularly the Germans and Swiss. The old swords had been designed for heavy swinging blows against an armored opponent. The rapier was a light thrusting sword, and its use became a fine art, called fencing, which every boy of noble birth was expected to learn. Duelling became fashionable, especially in France, and gentlemen were quick to defend their honor with their swords.

In Italy, where the art of fencing was first developed, sword and dagger were used together, the

GERMAN SOLDIER
WITH TWO-HANDED SWORD
from a 16th century woodcut

DAGGER WITH BRONZE SHEATH
Swiss, about 1570

sword in the right hand, the dagger in the left. The hilts of this rapier and its matching left-handed dagger are made of steel openwork in a tracery of twisting plants, strange birds, and dragons. The edge of the cup-shaped sword hilt, a better protection than the old form of guard, is turned back to catch the thrusting point of the enemy's rapier.

The heavy dagger above probably belonged to an officer in command of a company of Swiss soldiers. Its ornamented sheath, cast in bronze and then engraved and gilded, shows a scene from the legend of the Swiss hero, William Tell. You can see him kneeling at the narrow end of the sheath, his crossbow raised, ready to shoot the apple off the head of his son.

37

GERMAN SOLDIER
WITH MUSKET
from a 16th century woodcut

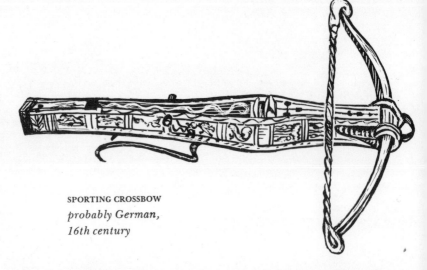

SPORTING CROSSBOW
probably German,
16th century

CRANEQUIN,
OR WINDER,
FOR CROSSBOW

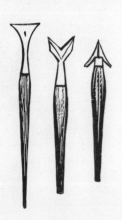

The crossbow was a powerful weapon. After the invention of firearms, crossbows were abandoned as weapons of war, but they were still useful for hunting. A sporting crossbow, like this one, was too strong to be bent by hand. Instead, the small *cranequin,* or winder, was fitted on the stock, and the metal claw hooked through the bowstring. As the bowman wound the handle, the string was pulled back and the bow was ready to be loaded with a bolt, a short thick arrow with an iron head. The bowman fired his bolt by squeezing the trigger underneath the stock to release the bowstring.

This crossbow was probably made for a nobleman. The stock is plated with white staghorn and engraved with scenes from the Book of Genesis, including Adam and Eve in the Garden of Eden.

CROSSBOW BOLTS
FOR HUNTING
German, about 1500

38

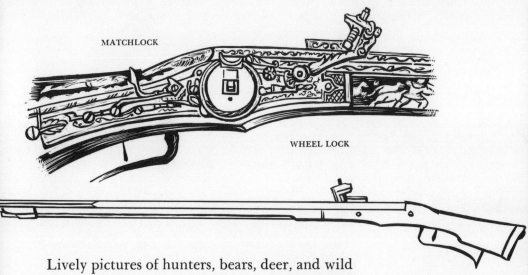

MATCHLOCK

WHEEL LOCK

HUNTING GUN
German, 1560

Lively pictures of hunters, bears, deer, and wild boars decorate the stock of this hunting gun, made for the Archduke Ferdinand of the Tyrol. The finest guns were made for use in sport, many of them by German craftsmen of Augsburg, Nuremberg and Munich. A hunting gun had to be beautiful to look at and also easy to aim and quick to fire. Much depended on the firing mechanism, the work of a locksmith. The Archduke's gun is fired by a wheel lock, but in case this should fail, it is also fitted with the older matchlock mechanism.

The earliest guns had been fired simply by touching a lighted match to the fine priming powder in the pan. With the Spanish invention of the matchlock, in the late fifteenth century, the slow-burning match was fastened to a small movable

39

HUNTSMAN WINDING UP A CROSSBOW
Detail from an engraved silver cup
English, 1611

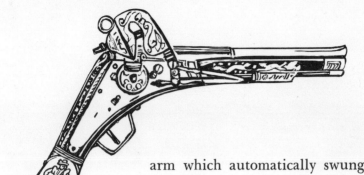

arm which automatically swung down onto the touchhole to ignite the powder when the trigger was pulled. The wheel lock did away with the awkward lighted match, so easily put out by wind or rain. In the new mechanism the small movable arm, or hammer, held a piece of iron pyrites. When the arm was pressed down into the firing position and the gunner pulled the trigger, a tiny metal wheel spun around against the iron pyrites, striking sparks which fell on the powder in the pan and fired the gun. Before firing again, the gunner had to wind up the wheel with a small key.

The invention of the wheel lock brought pistols into being. As these could be fired with one hand, they were usually made in pairs, and horse pistols, as they were called, were popular weapons for cavalry. Foot soldiers still used clumsy matchlock guns, so heavy that they had to be propped on a Y-shaped rest for firing. This musketeer carries the rest in his left hand, with the smoking match. The wooden cases hanging from his bandolier

MUSKETEER
early 17th century

40

each hold enough powder to charge his musket for one shot. Muskets were loaded through the muzzle with powder and ball, held down with a wad of paper, and even for well-drilled musketeers, the rate of fire was slow. The men were armed with swords to use when their guns were out of action, and in the line of battle they were protected by pikemen, like the one on page 42. Pikes were twelve to eighteen feet long, and when held horizontally by a determined band of pikemen, they confronted the enemy with a forest of steel points.

Halberds and other polearms were considerably shorter than pikes. Some, with blades richly engraved, were carried only in military processions; but the halberd was still a favorite weapon of the Swiss mercenary soldiers who hired themselves out to fight wherever an army was needed.

Ways of fighting had changed since the Middle Ages when knights rode into battle clad from head to foot in shining armor. To be proof against the new firearms, armor had to be made so heavy that a full suit of steel plates became a crippling weight. On the battlefield men took to wearing half-armor —little more than helmet and breastplate. But complete armor was still worn in tournaments and processions, and for these great occasions the armorers produced their finest work.

41

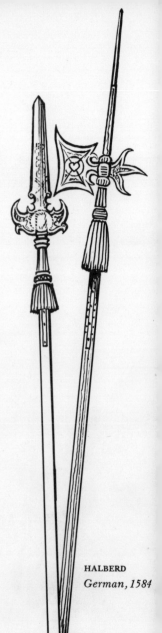

HALBERD
German, 1584

PARTISAN
German, 1615

SALLET
Venice, 1460

Armor

HE ARMOR OF RENAISSANCE PRINCES WAS as splendid as their dress. Painters, sculptors, and goldsmiths all shared in its design and decoration. The magnificent lion's head above, hammered out of copper and brilliantly gilded, covers a steel helmet called a sallet which protected the wearer's head and face down to his chin. The lion's mane curls down the back of the helmet, and the snarling mouth forms an eyepiece for the wearer to see through.

The German armor opposite actually follows the latest fashion in dress. Slashings and brocaded patterns are skillfully imitated in metal, and the visor of the helmet is shaped like the face of a warrior.

PIKEMAN
early 17th century

42

**MAXIMILIAN
ARMOR**
*Augsburg,
1510*

**GERMAN
COSTUME**
early 16th century

ARMORERS AT WORK

from a woodcut by
Hans Burgkmair
German, 16th century

This woodcut shows German armorers, employed by the Emperor Maximilian, hard at work

44

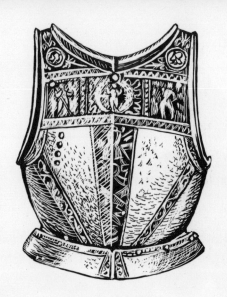

ETCHED BREASTPLATE
Milan, 1500

making fluted "Maximilian armor," which was decorated all over with the same thin ridges, or flutings, which you can see on some parts of the armor on page 43. The Emperor himself stands by the workbench, talking with his chief armorer, Conrad Seusenhofer. Beyond the furnace and huge bellows is a quantity of finished work — helmets, breastplates, and complete armors, or harnesses, as they were called.

Breastplates were decorated with special care. The Italian one above is etched with delicate drawings of the Christ Child, Saint Christopher, and Saint Sebastian, surrounded by patterns as rich as embroidery. Etching on armor was a new art, first practiced by Italian goldsmiths. It was

45

WEAPONS

Detail of etched design
on horse armor
Italian, 1575

ARMOR OF
THE EARL OF
CUMBERLAND
English,
1590-1595

done by coating the metal with varnish and scratching the design into the varnish with a sharp tool. Then the metal was put into a bath of acid which ate into the surface along the scratched lines and left the varnished parts in relief. German etchers often painted their designs in varnish on the bare metal and let the acid eat away the background, and some artists etched by both methods on the same piece of armor.

On the splendid harness at the left, etching and gilding have been used together to make a pattern of roses, lilies, and lovers' knots. This armor was made for George Clifford, Earl of Cumberland,

Above, KNEELING KNIGHT
Detail of etched design
on a breastplate
German, 1580

HELMET
*from parade
armor of Henry II
French, 1550*

by craftsmen at the royal armories of Queen Elizabeth I. One of these men drew this picture
in his notebook of designs for armor, in which
he also included a drawing of the Earl of Cumberland's suit. Each part of the Cumberland armor
is marked with a letter "E," in honor of the Queen.
The Earl served as her Champion, arranging entertainments at her royal residences, and his black-
and-gold armor must have made a brave show in
the pageants, processions, and tournaments so
much enjoyed by the Queen.

47

DESIGN FOR ARMOR
*from an armorer's album
English, late 16th century*

The helmet on page 47 is part of a wonderful suit of parade armor which belonged to Henry II, King of France. King Henry took after his father, Francis I, in his love of magnificence, and his helmet and armor are covered from top to toe with embossed designs of swirling leaves and scrolls, fighting warriors, serpents, masks, and sphinxes. All this decoration, standing out like sculpture in relief, was done by goldsmiths, working at the metal plates from underneath with small punches and hammers. Then the surface was gilded, damascened, and polished until the armor must have glittered in the sunshine when the King rode forth in triumph through the streets of Paris.

Horses were as sumptuously decked as their riders. The horse armor opposite, richly embossed and etched, bears the date 1548 and the initials of Johann Ernst, Duke of Saxony. It may have been worn when the Duke rode into Augsburg for a meeting of German princes, summoned in 1548 by the Emperor Charles V, son of Maximilian.

From armor belonging to the Emperor comes this tasset, which was fastened to the lower edge of the breastplate. It is adorned with a gilded griffin, the symbol of strength and vigilance. The Emperor was a great soldier; and, like most princes of his time, he celebrated his victories by triumphal

TASSET
from armor of Charles V
German, 1545

48

**ARMOR FOR
MAN AND HORSE**
German, 1548

RIDER IN PROCESSION
Detail from the
Triumphal Entry of
Charles V
German woodcut,
16th century

processions, in the style of the Caesars of ancient Rome. What a sight those Renaissance triumphs must have been! First would come trumpeters

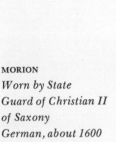

MORION
*Worn by State
Guard of Christian II
of Saxony
German, about 1600*

blowing fanfares; then soldiers on foot and on horseback, and knights and their chargers plumed with ostrich feathers. The prince himself might come riding on a splendid horse or enthroned upon a fantastic chariot, surrounded by his bodyguard in gilded helmets; and there would be great decorated wagons bearing trophies of victory, and bands of musicians, singers, and clowns.

Even the young pages in these processions wore ceremonial armor. The suit at the right, small enough to fit a boy, is covered with intricate designs chiseled into the metal and gilded, silvered, and damascened. Although full armor had become useless as a defense in battle, the skilled armorer still held a proud place among the many craftsmen who served the Renaissance princes.

51

PARADE ARMOR FOR A PAGE
Milan, 1610

Furniture and Decoration

COUNTRY HOUSE
Detail from the
painted decoration
of the virginal
shown on page 90
Flemish, 1581

HE GREAT HOUSES OF THE RENAISSANCE, like clothes and armor, were designed to display the wealth and power of their owners. They were no longer strongholds in the style of the grim castles of the Middle Ages, from which barons sallied forth to wage private wars against their neighbors. This elegant country house of the sixteenth century has no strong towers or battlements for defense. It is set in a delightful park; and the protective moat, which used to surround

52

the walls of a castle and could be crossed only by a drawbridge, has become a pleasant stretch of water where people go boating.

Houses like this one were as beautiful within as without. Lofty windows flooded the rooms with light, and decoration was on a grand scale, requiring the work of carpenters and sculptors, goldsmiths and locksmiths, painters, weavers, and embroiderers. Such great houses were not exclusively for noblemen. They were also the homes of rich merchants whose trains of pack horses, laden with goods, thronged the roads of Europe, and whose ships sailed into port with rich cargoes from the East and the New World. Flourishing trade brought luxuries unknown in the Middle Ages, and even in the modest houses of ordinary people, life was growing easier and more comfortable.

Among the most important furnishings of any household, large or small, were the chests, used for storing goods of all kinds. In wealthy Italian

CARVED FRIEZE
OF CUPIDS
from a marriage chest
Venice, late 16th century

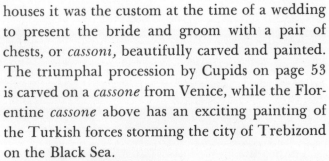

MARRIAGE CHEST
Florence, 1475

houses it was the custom at the time of a wedding to present the bride and groom with a pair of chests, or *cassoni,* beautifully carved and painted. The triumphal procession by Cupids on page 53 is carved on a *cassone* from Venice, while the Florentine *cassone* above has an exciting painting of the Turkish forces storming the city of Trebizond on the Black Sea.

German craftsmen, famous for all types of metalwork, made some of the best locks and hinges for chests and doors. These locksmiths also produced the first watches, as we have seen, and took delight in making wonderful clocks. This clock is in the form of the goddess Diana riding in a gilded chariot drawn by leopards. As the clock ticks, Diana rolls her eyes, and when it strikes the hour, all the figures spring into motion. The leopards nod; the

BRASS CANDLESTICK
German, 16th century

54

monkey sitting at Diana's right puts a fruit to his mouth; the bird hops up and down; and Diana raises her bow and shoots an arrow!

It is easy to understand why a character in Shakespeare's play, *Love's Labour's Lost,* speaks jokingly about:

> ". . . a German clock,
> Still a-repairing, ever out of frame,
> And never going aright . . ."

AUTOMATIC CLOCK
German, 16th century

BOX-CHAIR
English, about 1525
Right, CAQUETOIRE, OR GOSSIP
CHAIR *English, about 1535*

Fancy clocks were only for the rich, but everyone needed benches, stools, or chairs to sit on. The oak armchair at the left is made in the style of the Middle Ages, when chairs were large and throne-like, reserved for the lord and lady and their honored guests in the castle hall. Although Renaissance houses had great halls for ceremonial occasions, people also enjoyed the luxury of private

FALCONER
Detail from an embroidered
pillow-cover, English, 16th century

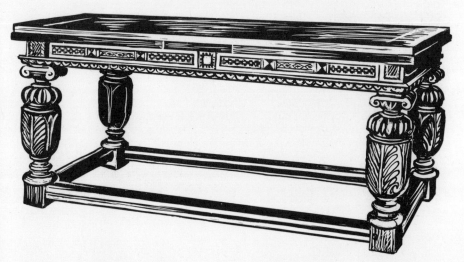

rooms where a few friends could meet and talk. Here we would find the small chairs which were coming into common use in the sixteenth century. The *caquetoire,* or "gossip chair," must have been specially designed for the ladies, chatting together over their embroidery; and for fashionable women, whose wide padded skirts made it hard for them to sit in a chair with arms, there was the convenient "farthingale chair," with its comfortable upholstered seat.

The making of dining tables was another sign of the new taste for luxury. In the Middle Ages, even in wealthy households, tables were simply boards laid on trestles, and cleared away when

DRAW-TABLE
English, about 1600

FARTHINGALE CHAIR
English, about 1615

not in use. The table on page 57 is a work of fine craftsmanship. Known as a draw-table, it can be almost doubled in length by drawing out two extra leaves from under the top. The richly carved legs and the patterns of inlaid wood around the top would probably have been hidden under a heavy table carpet in the seventeenth century. Oriental rugs, far too precious to be spread on the floor, were often used as table covers; and embroidered covers were made at home by the same skilled needlewomen whose work we have seen in costumes.

The view of a country estate, with men out fishing, shooting, and hunting, must have been a familiar sight for the women who embroidered it

58

on the border of an English table carpet. The center of the carpet has a close-knit design of grape-vines, and the whole work is done in tent stitch, with about four hundred stitches to the square inch.

Great carved beds, with their embroidered hangings, coverlets, and pillowcases, were treasured

59

ELEPHANT
Detail from an embroidered
pillow-cover
English, 16th century

family heirlooms, passed down from father to son; and in small households the best bed was often proudly displayed in the parlor. Beds were the largest and costliest furniture in any house, and the famous Great Bed of Ware, now in the Victoria and Albert Museum in London, is big enough to hold twelve people!

The embroiderers adorned these wonderful beds with appropriate splendor. The curtains and the fringed valance around the top were sewn with colored silks, gold and silver thread, and sometimes pearls. Covers for pillows, especially those worked by English needlewomen, had gay designs of birds, flowers, animals, coats of arms, and scenes from the Bible. The picture of Noah's Ark is one of four illustrations for the story of Noah embroidered on a linen pillow cover. The needlewoman probably copied the pictures from woodcuts in an illustrated Bible, tracing every detail with the

GENTLEMAN *Detail from an*
embroidered silk panel
French, 16th century

60

THE ANIMALS ENTER THE ARK *Detail from an embroidered pillow-cover, English, about 1600*

greatest care, from the peacock on the roof of the Ark to the spiny hedgehog on the ground below.

The embroidered pictures so popular in France were generally worked by professional craftsmen. Rooms in the great French châteaux were decorated with sets of these needlework pictures, covering tables, chairs, stools, and beds; and on the walls were embroidered hangings and fine tapestries.

The bagpiper comes from a tapestry of country scenes, woven in Flanders. Tapestries showing peasants at work and play were as fashionable in the early sixteenth century as those with scenes from courtly life, in which ladies and gentlemen strolled through flowery meadows or made music in the

61

BAGPIPER
Detail from a tapestry
Flemish, early 16th century

open air. Later in the century tapestries grew more grandiose and complicated in color and design. They illustrated events of current history, stories from the Bible, and classical myths. Tapestry weavers and embroiderers often worked from designs by famous artists, and they became so skilled in their crafts that they could imitate, in threads of silk and wool, silver and gold, the subtle effects of painting.

Another favorite way of decorating rooms, particularly small ones, was by lining the walls with wood paneling, or "wainscot." This little paneled room was originally a study in the palace of Duke Federigo da Montefeltro, the wise ruler of Urbino in northern Italy. At first sight it seems as though there are benches along the sides of the room and cupboards in the walls above. The latticed cupboard doors seem to stand open, inviting us to reach in and touch the many things inside. A second look shows that the walls are really flat and solid; the benches and cupboards are pictures made from inlaid wood of varied grains and colors. The whole room is meant to fool the eye by the wonderful skill of the woodworkers who made the panels, and by the designer's brilliant use of mathematical perspective, a new science which thrilled the Italian artists of the day.

CITTERN, HOUR-GLASS,
DIVIDERS AND LEVEL
*from the inlaid paneling
of the study*

Duke Federigo himself was a student of science; and scientific instruments, such as the hourglass, pair of dividers, and triangular level, are pictured in the cupboards around his study. The cittern

and thirteen other musical instruments are proof of his love of music, and weapons and armor remind us of his prowess as a soldier in wars and tournaments. In the cupboard by the window is a parakeet in a cage, a bird from the distant tropics, showing the Duke's curiosity about the exploration of far lands; and all around the room we find books from his great library, in which the writings of the early fathers of the Church were mingled with pagan classics of ancient Greece and Rome.

A copy of Virgil's *Aeneid* is pictured just as the Duke might have left it, lying open on a reading stand. This thrilling epic poem was a favorite

64

among Latin classics. The lord of a French château loved the book so well that he decorated one of his rooms with sixty-nine enamel plaques to illustrate the story. This one shows Aeneas and his followers, in fifteenth-century costume, sailing to the shores of Italy. The designs for the plaques were copied from woodcuts in a German edition of the *Aeneid,* printed in 1502; and the enamelwork, in jewel-like colors, was done by craftsmen of Limoges, a French town long famous for fine enamels.

Plaques such as these were often set into wood paneling, which might also be richly carved. This oak panel comes from a room in an English manor house. Here the round portrait of the owner of the house shows us the new fashion for portrait sculpture, which began in Italy and was inspired, as we shall see, by the exciting rediscovery of the art of ancient Rome.

CARVED WOOD PANEL
WITH A PORTRAIT
IN RELIEF
English, 1546

MARBLE BUST OF
PHILIP II OF SPAIN
by Leone Leoni
Italian, 16th century

Sculpture

HE PEOPLE OF THE RENAISSANCE SHARED with the Romans a great love of portraits. Princes and noble ladies, merchants, lawyers, Churchmen, and explorers were proud of themselves and their achievements. They wanted to be remembered in years to come by having their portraits painted, carved in wood or stone, modeled in clay, or cast in enduring bronze.

Some portraits were large and majestic; others, as we have seen, were tiny miniatures to be worn as jewelry. Scores of small bronze medals, bearing the portraits of famous people, were made in the fifteenth and sixteenth centuries, often to commemorate great historical events — weddings, state

BRONZE MEDAL: FRANCIS,
DUKE OF VALOIS, AFTERWARDS
FRANCIS I OF FRANCE
by Giovanni Candida, Italian, 1450-1504

66

visits, or victories in war. The design of these little bronze portraits was copied from the profiles of emperors on Roman coins, which were the commonest relics to be found among the ruins of ancient Rome. Within a diameter of less than four inches, a Florentine sculptor gives us this fine portrait of Lorenzo de' Medici, the great ruler of Florence, who had earned the name of The Magnificent by his generosity and the splendor of his life. Lorenzo was one of the first collectors of ancient Roman sculpture, and his palace was a meeting place for poets, scholars and artists.

Sculptors adopted the Roman idea of carving portrait busts, and in the marble bust of Philip II of Spain, the rival of Queen Elizabeth I, the sculptor has even clothed the King in Roman armor and a drapery like a toga.

67

BRONZE FIGURE OF SAINT JOHN
from a Crucifixion
Italian, 1480-1500

HEAD OF FRANCIS I
French, about 1529

The elegant portrait of Francis I, the work of a French sculptor, is not carved in marble but made of terra cotta, or "baked clay," covered with a smooth white glaze. This material had long been used for making pottery, but Luca della Robbia of Florence was the first to use glazed clay for sculpture. He was a religious sculptor, so busy with orders for his statues and reliefs that he had to give up carving in marble for the quicker work of modeling in clay. He found he could give his clay figures the beauty of marble by coating them with a glaze of white enamel, made from sand and molten tin. After the whitened clay had been baked, he painted it with colored glazes of rich blue, yellow, green, and violet, and fixed them by a second firing in the kiln. It took him years of toil and experiment to perfect his method, and

SAINT JOHN THE BAPTIST AS A BOY
by Giovanni della Robbia
Florentine, late 15th century

68

ADORATION
*by Andrea della Robbia
Florentine,
late 15th century*

before he died, at the ripe age of eighty-five, he taught his difficult art to his nephew Andrea, who made this lovely relief of the Virgin and Child. Andrea's twelve children must often have served him as models for the Christ Child and the small winged cherubs in his sculptures. His four sons grew up to carry on the family craft; and one of them, Giovanni, made the bust of John the Baptist, showing the saint as a serious young boy.

The busy workshop of the della Robbias was one of many artists' shops, or *bottegas,* in fifteenth-century Florence. The whole city was buzzing

69

THE VIRGIN WITH
THE LAUGHING CHILD
by Antonio Rossellino
Florentine, about 1465

with new ideas in art. Florentine sculptors were deep in the study of human anatomy, as thrilling as the new science of perspective; but they also loved the bustling life of their city, the pageants and processions in the streets, and the crowds of people, great and small. Antonio Rossellino, who made the terra-cotta statue of the Virgin and Child, was a great admirer of the work of Luca della Robbia. Antonio usually worked in marble, carving fine portraits as well as figures of saints. This little statue, as lifelike as any portrait, was probably meant to be a sketch for a larger sculpture in marble.

The terra-cotta bust of Henry VII, King of Eng-

71

land, was made by another Florentine, Pietro Torrigiano. There is no flattery in this portrait of the King. It shows Henry VII as he really was, a stern, cautious man who built England into a strong kingdom for his brilliant son, Henry VIII.

Torrigiano himself must have been a man of fiery temper. He quarreled with the great sculptor, Michelangelo, broke his opponent's nose in a fist fight, and was forced to leave Italy as a result, for Michelangelo was a favorite of the powerful Medici family. Traveling to England, Torrigiano brought with him the Italian style of sculpture and decoration, and was summoned to the court of Henry VII to make a bronze bust of the King, which is now in Westminster Abbey.

Bronze was used for sculptures of all sizes. Wealthy men collected little bronze figures, portrait medals and plaques, and some sculptors specialized in the casting of small bronzes.

This was anxious and difficult work. Having made a clay model of the figure he wanted to cast, the sculptor copied it in wax which was spread in a thin coating over an inner core of clay. He covered the finished wax model with a thick layer of clay to form the mold, and when this was heated, the wax melted and ran out through little holes. Then the molten metal was poured into the mold,

BRONZE MEDAL: LOUIS XIII OF FRANCE
AS A BOY, IN THE FIRST YEAR OF HIS REIGN
by Guillaume Dupré, French, 1610

72

BRONZE COCK
Florentine, 1625-1650

filling all the space where the wax had been, and the bronze was left to cool and set. At last the mold could be broken away, and if the casting had gone well, the hardened metal appeared in the exact shape of the wax model, needing only to be smoothed, polished, and possibly gilded.

This noble bronze cock shows how carefully the Florentine sculptor who made it had studied the anatomy of the bird, its bone structure, and the pattern of the feathers. The ugly little monster, on the other hand, has no likeness to any animal, living or dead, and by giving it a gaping mouth and a handle, the sculptor has made it into an unusual water jug for a rich man's table.

73

BRONZE JUG
North Italian,
late 16th century

MAJOLICA DISH
Italian, about 1515-1520

Tableware

SHOW OF FINE TABLEWARE WAS THE pride of a Renaissance household. The best plates and serving dishes, jugs and wine cups were prominently displayed, often on a special set of shelves called a court cupboard; and of all the tableware, made of pottery, glass, wood, or metal, the most colorful was Italian majolica.

The secret of its beauty was in the painted decoration, usually done in brilliant shades of yellow, blue, and warm orange. When the piece of pottery

POTTER WORKING
AT HIS WHEEL

74

COURT CUPBOARD FOR
DISPLAYING TABLEWARE
English,
late 16th century

had been shaped on the potter's wheel, it was
coated with a white tin glaze like that used by
Luca della Robbia for his sculptures. The painter
put on the design while the glaze was still wet. He
had to work swiftly and without mistakes, for it
was impossible to make any corrections. Then the
piece was fired in the kiln to fix the glaze and the
colors, and sometimes, by a second firing, it was
given the added beauty of an iridescent luster.

The splendid dish, with its picture of a hound
attacking a deer, was made at the Italian town of
Deruta, and the small jug comes from Gubbio,
where the Dukes of Urbino were patrons of the
potters. Majolica was made in many towns of Italy,

75

MAJOLICA JUG
Italian, about 1520-1530

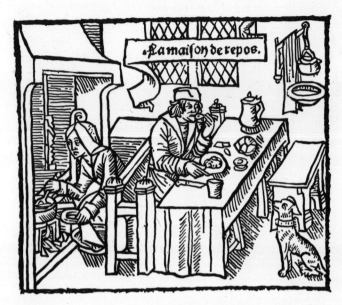

COOKING AND
EATING SUPPER
from a woodcut in
Le Chasteau de Labour
Paris, 1505

and traveling Italian potters taught the craftsmen of northern Europe the art of making tin-glazed pottery.

The majestic drinking vessel, in the shape of an owl with a removable head, is the work of a potter of Nuremberg where these blue-and-white owl cups were popular as presents. This one may have been made for a German prince, the Elector of Brandenburg, whose coat of arms adorns the shield on the owl's breast.

For ordinary people the German potters made practical brown earthenware, with decorations in

JUG: GERMAN EARTHENWARE
WITH ENGLISH SILVER MOUNTS
about 1580

76

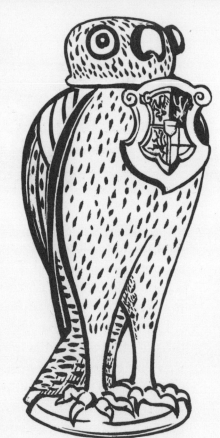

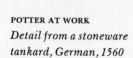

relief. One potter molded a figure of himself among the raised designs on a tall tankard for beer, and on the squat brown jug at the right is a pattern of leafy branches and the face of a bearded man. German earthenware was exported to England, but the jugs were too plain for English taste. Many of them were given silver covers and bases

77

EARTHENWARE JUG
German, about 1540

CHINESE PORCELAIN BOWL
WITH SILVER MOUNTS
1573-1619

by English goldsmiths. Finely wrought silver mounts were also made for bowls and jugs of precious porcelain from China, and glossy brown coconuts from Far Eastern shores were mounted in silver as handsome cups.

Chinese bowls, like this one which has been fitted with silver handles in the shape of mermaids, were bought by Portuguese merchants at the port of Macao in China and shipped to Europe by the long sea route of Vasco da Gama, across the Indian Ocean and around the Cape of Good Hope. Portugal was the center for trade with the Far East in the sixteenth century, as Venice had been during the Middle Ages. Porcelain had first been brought to Europe from China by the great Venetian traveler, Marco Polo, in the thirteenth century, and by 1470 the skilled potters of Venice had learned to make their own porcelain, in imitation of the Chinese. But far more famous than

COCONUT CUP
WITH SILVER MOUNTS
English, about 1580

78

GLASS COVERED CUP
IN GERMAN STYLE
Venice, about 1500

Venetian porcelain was the wonderful Venetian glass. The glassworkers ranked above all other craftsmen in the city. Their work was in demand as far away as England, where Henry VIII had a great collection of Venetian glass. Some of the glassware was specially designed for export, and tall covered cups of impressive size, made in the German style, must have had a place of honor on the banquet tables of German princes.

79

CHINESE PORCELAIN WINE JUG
MOUNTED IN SILVER-GILT
London, 1585

WINEGLASS
Venice,
early 17th century

There were glassworks in other cities, both in Italy and northern Europe, but no one could make glass like the Venetians. The secrets of their craft were jealously guarded. The glassworkers were forced, by order of their city, to live and work on the island of Murano, a short distance from Venice, and were threatened with death if they tried to escape.

They labored night and day in the heat of their furnaces. Some men produced window glass and bottles, and others, brightly patterned glass beads; but the most skillful of all were the makers of tableware. The precious glass, mixed by secret formulas, was melted in clay pots arranged around the fire in the dome-shaped furnace. The glass blower would reach into the furnace, through one of the small windows, and gather a lump of molten glass on the end of his long blowing pipe. He lightly rolled the glass into a round shape on a stone slab and sometimes lengthened it out by swinging the blowing pipe around his head. Then he blew into the pipe and watched the lump of glass swell up like a small balloon.

When he had blown it to the proper size, he took it off the pipe and shaped the globe of glass with shears and pincers. To make a wine cup, he attached a round base and, perhaps, a delicate

ENAMELED GLASS GOBLET
Venice, about 1575

80

twisted stem. He might apply spots of colored glass
as a decoration, as you can see on the cup on page
79; or, when the work had cooled and hardened,
it could be painted with enamel made from melted glass, gum arabic, and metallic dyes. About
1500 the craftsmen developed a clear white glass,
too beautiful to be covered by paint, and heavy
enameling passed out of fashion. The goblet at
the right, made in England in the Venetian style,
is adorned with engravings done with a diamond.
This was a popular art for amateur craftsmen, and
some noble ladies were expert engravers, using

81

WINEGLASS IN VENETIAN STYLE
English, 1602

SILVER FORK
*from a set
of knife, fork
and spoon
Rome, about 1580*

finger rings, like the one on page 30, set with sharply pointed "writing diamonds."

From Italy, along with glass and majolica, came more refined table manners and the custom of using forks at meals. This silver fork, with a matching knife and spoon, was designed for the personal use of its owner when dining at home or as a guest. It had long been the custom for guests to provide their own table knives. The man in the woodcut on page 76 eats his supper with knife and spoon, the common practice until the seventeenth century. Hanging on the wall behind him are a basin, towel, and pot of water for hand-washing before a meal. The man spoons his stew from a dish which is probably made of wood. Even in rich men's houses, plates of wood, pewter, and tin were used for everyday. Among the Elizabethan gentry, who were hearty eaters of meat, game, and "potato pyes," it was usual to finish a meal by serving up cheese and fruit on gaily painted trenchers of beechwood, with patterns of fruit and flowers, or moral inscriptions.

On great occasions the dinner tables of the rich glittered with silver and gold. One of the most

BEECHWOOD FRUIT
TRENCHER *from a set
of twelve trenchers
English, about 1615*

82

STANDING SALT KNOWN
AS THE VYVYAN SALT
English, 1592

elaborate items of tableware was the splendid con-
tainer for salt, which marked the division between
the honored guests, who sat "above the salt," and
the less important ones below. This tall "Standing
Salt," of silver-gilt, is crowned with a figure of

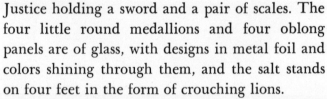

Justice holding a sword and a pair of scales. The four little round medallions and four oblong panels are of glass, with designs in metal foil and colors shining through them, and the salt stands on four feet in the form of crouching lions.

In the sixteenth century, when Spanish ships were sailing home from the New World laden with treasure, silver became so common in Europe that many people could afford to use shining silver tableware. The goldsmiths who made it were flourishing as never before, and by 1563, in the city of Rouen alone, there were two hundred and sixty-five master goldsmiths!

The powerful goldsmiths' guilds kept a strict eye on their members and made sure that no one outside the guild should work with precious metals. As most goldsmiths' work was in silver, gilded with gold leaf, dishonest craftsmen might cheat by gilding base metal, such as copper. Each finished piece of work had to be weighed and

84

tested for the purity of the metal and stamped with the special mark of the guild, known in London as the "hallmark" because it was stamped on at the guild's headquarters, the Goldsmiths' Hall.

This slender wine cup bears the London hallmark. You can see a similar cup in the woodcut, which shows servants unpacking a picnic for a royal hunting party, complete with hampers of cooked capons and tall jugs of wine.

Goldsmiths excelled in the making of wine cups. The lovely columbine cup, with its bowl shaped like a flower, was made by a craftsman of Nuremberg and submitted to the heads of his guild as his "masterpiece," to prove that he was worthy of

SILVER-GILT WINE CUP
London, 1603

FOOD AND DRINK FOR A ROYAL HUNTING PARTY
Detail from an illustration in The Noble Arte of Venerie or Hunting by George Turberville, London, 1611

the rank of master craftsman. This form of cup had been chosen by the guild as a severe test of the skill of the craftsman. There can be no doubt that this man passed the test. His cup is a miracle of fine workmanship. Four strange figures seem to grow out of the stem; embossed around the bottom of the bowl are six little boys representing the arts and sciences; and engraved around the top are six scenes from the Old Testament.

There was no limit to the fantastic design of cups. The frontispiece of this book shows a covered cup in the form of a noble stag. The cover is the stag's head and neck, divided from the body by the collar. Another covered cup is this little astronomical globe, held on the shoulders of a goat-legged satyr and engraved with the constellations of the night sky.

Coiled nautilus shells, brought home from tropical seas, were mounted as cups, and shell cups were carved from rare amber gathered on the shores of the Baltic. Perhaps the most wonderful cup of all is this one, which some say was made by Benvenuto Cellini. Whether or not he made it with his own hands, it is worthy of his art. Only a goldsmith of genius could have made this golden scallop shell, supported by a blue-green enameled dragon on the back of a golden tortoise, and placed

COVERED CUP
German, 1560-1600

on the shell the brilliant winged sphinx with tiny pearls dangling from its ears.

This cup must have been proudly displayed among the dishes of gold and silver on a prince's table, gleaming in the light of many candles and surrounded by guests in glowing silks and velvets; while the household musicians, indispensable at a time of feasting and celebration, filled the scented air with the melody of lutes, harps, and viols.

THE ROSPIGLIOSI CUP
possibly by
Benvenuto Cellini
Italian,
16th century

87

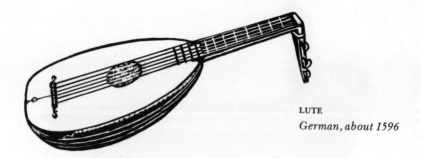

LUTE
German, about 1596

Musical Instruments

THERE WAS MUSIC EVERYWHERE IN THE Renaissance — in palaces, cottages, and churches, and even aboard the ships of the explorers. Country people danced and sang to the music of homemade pipes and drums, and in the towns skilled craftsmen made instruments of such beauty that princes and noblemen collected them as works of art.

The soft-voiced lute, plucked like the modern guitar, was the instrument most highly prized for solo playing or for accompanying a singer. Lutes were sometimes made of ivory or of rare brazil-wood from the New World. In the woodcut of the Emperor's instruments, the lute is enclosed in a

TROMBONE PLAYER

large case behind the drums and trombone. The man in the center of the picture plays a harp, which was almost as popular as the lute, and next to him is a small portable organ with one man at the keyboard and another to work the bellows. The box-shaped instrument on the table is a virginal, ancestor of the harpsichord and piano. The

THE EMPEROR MAXIMILIAN
AND HIS COLLECTION OF
MUSICAL INSTRUMENTS
Detail from a woodcut
by Hans Burgkmair
German, 16th century

89

MVSICA · DVLCE · LABORVM · LEVAMEN

strings of the virginal were not struck with hammers, as in the piano, but plucked with little quills, or jacks, to make light twanging notes.

Queen Elizabeth I was a gifted performer on the virginal. Her instruments must have been as beautiful as the one above, which was made by Hans Ruckers of Antwerp, the founder of a famous family of harpsichord makers. This instrument is really two in one, for the left-hand keyboard belongs to a little octave spinet which can be pulled out like a drawer and played separately. The long case is decorated with inlaid wood, and inside the lid is a painting of a favorite pastime of the Renaissance — a musical garden party in the grounds of a country house.

BASS VIOLA DA GAMBA
by Giovanni Batista Ciciliano
Venice, about 1550

PLAYING A
VIOLA DA GAMBA

Every educated person was expected to be able
to read music, sing in part songs, and play an instrument. The viola da gamba was specially suited
to playing in groups, and many composers wrote
music for a consort, or family, of four viols —
soprano, alto, tenor, and bass. The viols were
given the name of gamba, the Italian for "leg,"

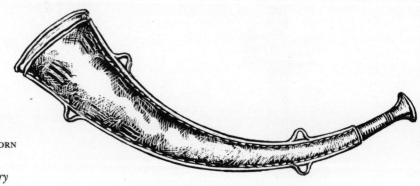

because of the way they were played. The smaller, higher-pitched viols rested on the player's knees, while larger ones were held between the legs. Another popular instrument at musical parties was the recorder, made and played in consorts like the viols. It was the most important member of the flute family, and Henry VIII, a fine musician and composer, had seventy-six recorders of varying sizes.

The Italians considered stringed instruments to be far nobler than brasses or woodwinds, largely because wind players, with their puffed-out cheeks, looked so undignified. Yet no music could be as thrilling as a fanfare of trumpets to call an army into battle or to herald the approach of a king.

No occasion of ceremony was complete without music; and, just as princes had their household musicians, each city had its town band. Ships set forth to the sound of music, and some of the

PLAYING
RECORDERS

92

town musicians of Norwich accompanied Sir Francis Drake on one of his voyages. The navigator John Davis had four musicians among his men when he set sail with two small ships, the *Sunshine* and the *Moonshine*, in search of the Northwest Passage to the East. Going ashore on an island off the Greenland coast, Davis found the Eskimos especially hostile, and the *Moonshine*'s boat put out to rescue him with the four musicians. At Davis's command, they struck up a lively jig. He and his men began to dance, and quickly won the friendship of the astonished Eskimos.

Dancing was the delight of rich and poor. William Kemp, an actor of Shakespeare's time, danced all the way from London to Norwich and wrote a book about his escapade, called the *Nine Daies' Wonder*. Country people danced on the village green, while kings and queens performed intricate court dances, such as the sprightly galliard and majestic pavane. Dancing was a necessary part of the education of children of noble birth. They grew up in a world of music, and even when they rode out to hunt, the shrill music of the hunting horn echoed before them down the green glades of the forest.

93

TRUMPETER
Detail from the
Triumphal Entry of Charles V
German woodcut, 16th century

HUNTSMAN
from a playing card
Dutch, 17th century

Sports and Games

CTIVE SPORTS WERE AS IMPORTANT AS music in the education of young noblemen of the Renaissance. Boys learned early how to use crossbow and longbow, sword and dagger, and how to ride a horse with grace and skill. Hunting on horseback was the sport of kings and nobles. Over their wide estates they hunted the hare, the wild boar, and the stag. A royal staghunt was a ceremonial affair. Huntsmen and hounds went on ahead to seek out the finest stag, and an elaborate hunt breakfast was served in the forest before the stag was roused from the covert and the gallant chase began. Henry VIII is said to have worn out

Above, GAME WITH MECHANICAL TOYS
Left, LONGBOW AND CROSSBOW
Details from a woodcut by
Hans Burgkmair, German, 16th century

94

HUNTING THE STAG *Detail from the border of the Bradford Table-carpet English, late 16th century*

ten horses in a single day of hunting, and Queen Elizabeth I took after him in her love of the chase. She also enjoyed falconry, and the falconer below is one of a party out hawking with the Queen. He looses from his gloved fist a peregrine falcon, swift as an arrow, to bring down a heron in flight.

Among warlike sports was the art of jousting, or single combat with a lance. In the woodcut opposite the boys are playing at jousting with little mechanical figures, armed and equipped like knights in a tournament. The horses are covered by flowing draperies and bulky padding, and the men wear heavy helms protecting face and head. Long, blunted lances are held under their right arms, and one of the knights has almost unhorsed his opponent with a well-aimed blow.

Jousts and tournaments between medieval knights were sometimes fought to the death, but in the Renaissance jousting had become a game,

95

FALCONER *Detail from an illustration in The Booke of Faulconrie by George Turberville London, 1575*

GAME OF BOWLS *from a Flemish manuscript calendar, early 16th century*

controlled by strict rules. Tournaments were less like battles than splendid pageants. They were usually held on state occasions, such as the famous meeting of Henry VIII and Francis I at the Field of the Cloth of Gold. Here, before their camps of silken tents and gold pavilions, the two kings met in friendly combat, and Henry VIII was unhorsed, which did not improve his relations with the King of France!

Both kings were proud of their skill in sports, and Francis I was a particularly fine tennis player. Bowls, like tennis, was a popular sport in town and country. Sir Francis Drake was playing bowls at Plymouth when he heard of the coming of the Spanish Armada — and calmly finished his game before making ready for battle.

Chess and cards were favorite indoor games. Chess had been played in Europe since the early days of the Middle Ages, but cards were a comparatively recent invention. The first card game,

PLAYING CARD:
QUEEN OF HEARTS
French, 16th century

96

IVORY CHESS MAN
German, 16th century

PLAYING CARD:
NINE OF RABBITS
German, about 1470

tarocco, probably originated in Italy in the 1300's.
By 1450 people all over Europe, rich and poor,
were gambling away their money at games of cards.

The pictures on the cards varied from one country to another. The French were the first to mark
the four suits of the pack with the familiar hearts,
diamonds, spades, and clubs. The German cardmakers used a great assortment of symbols, including knives and frying pans, and they even made
round cards in five suits — rabbits, parrots, carna-
tions, columbines, and roses. The sailor comes

97

PAINTED TAROCCO CARD
Italian,
15th century

from a Dutch pack with pictures of men of different trades, accompanied by their wives.

The cards on this page are woodcuts, the sailor in black and white and the king colored by hand. The earliest cards were drawn and painted entirely by hand, like miniatures in medieval manuscripts, but the cardmakers needed a quicker, cheaper method. About 1450 they began to cut their designs in relief on blocks of hard wood, spread them with ink, and print them on paper. Popular pictures of saints were already being made in this way, and woodcuts were very soon to be used as illustrations in printed books.

Left, SAILOR
Dutch playing card,
17th century
Right, KING OF DIAMONDS
French playing card,
16th century

Books and Printing

HE INVENTION OF PRINTING FROM MOV-
able type was a discovery as exciting
as Columbus's first sight of the New
World. These six lines of Latin text
come from a page of the first great
printed book, the Gutenberg Bible, published in
the German city of Mainz in 1456. Johann Gutenberg designed the book to look like the hand-
written books of his time. He took the forms of
the letters from the Gothic script used by scribes,
but instead of being written with a pen, each letter
was printed from a separate piece of type, cast in
metal. Instead of a single copy of the Bible, taking
months of labor to write by hand, a hundred
copies could be made at the same time, simply by
pressing together paper and inked type.

99

KING
Illustration from the
Nuremberg Chronicle, 1493

Left, PAPERMAKER
from a woodcut by
Jost Amman
German, 16th century
Right, PRINTING PRESS
Printer's mark of
Jodocus Badius
Paris, 1507

Some of Gutenberg's Bibles were printed on vellum, or calfskin, the usual material for manuscripts, but paper provided a far better surface for printing, as Gutenberg must have known. Paper could also be made in larger quantities than parchment and vellum, which were laboriously prepared from the skins of animals. Papermakers were as important as printers in producing the flood of printed books which followed Gutenberg's invention.

The paper was made from rags mixed with water and beaten to a pulp with large hammers, first worked by hand and later by water power.

100

Through the back window of the paper mill, you can see the tops of the water wheels, turned by the force of the millstream. In the foreground is a large vat of pulp. The papermaker picks up a thin sheet of the pulp on a framework of parallel wires. When some of the water has drained away through the wires, he will slide the sheet off the frame and put it between felt cloths under the press to squeeze it dry. The press, which stands behind him, is worked by a big screw, in exactly the same way as a printing press.

Besides having ten to twenty presses, a large printing house of the sixteenth century included a foundry where the type was cast. Many letters were needed for a book, and the type casters spent several weeks making type before the compositor could begin to set up the pages. The compositor is sitting at the right in the picture. With two pages of manuscript before him as a guide, he sets the text, a line at a time, in the composing stick in his hand. Each line will then be transferred to a framework called a form, the same size as the page, and when the form is filled, it will be handed over to the men at the press.

The man with the two leather "ink balls" spreads on the type the rich black ink, made of lampblack or powdered charcoal mixed with

BORDER OF FLOWERS
from a Book of Hours
printed by Geoffroy Tory
Paris, 1527

linseed oil. The paper is damped to get a clearer and blacker impression, and the second man puts type and paper on the press, sliding them into place with a turn of the little handle at the side of the press bed. Then he seizes the large handle in both hands and hauls down the screw to print a proof of the page.

The first proofs were read by a corrector and the type reset where necessary to take out mistakes. Correctors were usually learned scholars; but, in the great printing house of Christophe Plantin in Antwerp, the printer's five daughters all worked at correcting proofs in several languages before they were twelve years old. They were supposed to start at the age of four, but their father remarked that Henriette, the youngest, was slow. She was eight and still unable to correct proofs!

When the pages of a book had been printed, they were sent to a bookbinder, who was often the owner of a bookshop. Most books were sold in

plain covers of leather or parchment, but decorated bindings were made for the libraries of kings
and rich scholars. This handsome book cover of
red morocco leather was made in Venice for Queen
Elizabeth I. It is adorned with gold tooling, an art
which Venetian craftsmen had learned from the
Arabs. Venice had been the home of fine printing
and bookmaking since 1469, when the art of printing had been introduced there by a German craftsman, John of Speyer.

103

TEACHER AND CLASS
from the title page of
Opus Grammatica
Venice, about 1495

This picture of scholars, young and old, appears on the title page of a well-known Latin grammar book, published in Venice and used in schools as far away as England. Latin was a vital subject in school, and educated boys, and sometimes girls as well, were expected to read and speak Latin at an early age. Many schoolboys must have read the poems of Virgil in the small cheap edition published in 1501 by Aldus Manutius, one of the most learned Venetian printers. Manutius was famous for his pocket-size volumes of Latin classics, cheap enough for poor scholars to buy, and he was one of the first to print books in Greek.

AL DVS

PRINTER'S MARK OF
ALDUS MANUTIUS
Venice, 1520

104

Manutius' books were bound in fine tooled leather, but most of them had little decoration inside. He knew that scholars wanted an accurate text, plain and unadorned; while rich booklovers, who liked well-illustrated books, found printed pictures a poor substitute for the miniatures in manuscripts. Duke Federigo of Urbino would have no printed books in his great library, and for fourteen years he kept thirty scribes at work in his palace, copying out Greek and Latin books. The battle scene above comes from a manuscript of

PYRRHUS' LAST FIGHT
from a miniature in
Plutarch's Lives
Italian manuscript,
1460-1470

105

Plutarch's *Lives*, probably made for a North Italian prince. The book contains Latin translations of ten of the biographies of great men of Greece and Rome, originally written by Plutarch in Greek in the first century A.D. Plutarch's book was also translated into Italian; and from the English version of the *Lives*, made by Sir Thomas North and published in 1579, Shakespeare took the plot of his play, *Julius Caesar*.

Although the making of books by hand was too slow and costly to compete against printing, scribes and illuminators produced some of their loveliest work in the fifteenth and sixteenth centuries. Prayer books for private use, known as Books of Hours because they provided prayers for different hours of the day, were richly adorned with miniatures and flowery borders in bright colors and shining gold. Paris was especially famous for these books, and it was a Parisian printer and wood engraver, named Philip Pigouchet, who ventured to publish the first printed Book of Hours. The design of dancing shepherds on page 102 is typical of the lively pictures which filled the margins of Pigouchet's books. His experiment was a success and many beautiful Books of Hours, decorated with woodcuts, were printed in Paris in the early sixteenth century.

HYACINTH
from a Latin herbal by
Petrus Andreas Matthiolus
1598

The people of the Renaissance, like those of the Middle Ages, were fond of gardens and keenly interested in the medicinal uses of flowers and herbs. Travelers and explorers often brought home strange plants, such as the potato from South America, to be carefully nurtured in European gardens. A new enthusiasm arose for the science of botany, and books on flowers and gardening had a place in every gentleman's library.

Sport was an equally serious subject among the gentry, and the Elizabethans must have welcomed *The Booke of Faulconrie* and *The Noble Arte of Venerie or Hunting*, first published in 1575 and filled with valuable information on hawks, hounds, and the proper conduct of the chase.

STAG AT BAY
from The Noble Arte of Venerie or Hunting London, 1611

BOOKSHOP IN PARIS
*Detail from an
engraving by
Abraham Bosse
French, 1637*

There were stories for light reading, and in this small French bookshop the shopkeeper's wife is showing her customer a romance written in verse.

Travelers' tales had always been popular, and in printed books they reached a bigger audience than ever before. People longed to know about the strange life and customs of distant lands, and Marco Polo's story of his travels in the Far East, a

108

favorite since the Middle Ages, held a new magic for Renaissance readers. Columbus and John Cabot both read this famous book before sailing westward in search of the riches of the East. Their calculations of the size of the earth and the positions of China and Japan were based on Marco Polo's account of Cathay and Cipangu and the fabulous empire of Kublai Khan.

A far more accurate estimate of the earth's size could be found in the first world atlas, the *Geographia* of Claudius Ptolemy, who lived in Egypt in the second century A.D. and whose writings had been forgotten for more than a thousand years. Ptolemy had mapped the world as far as it was known in his day and devised the system of latitude and longitude. In the many printed editions of his book, the new findings of the explorers were added to Ptolemy's maps, as you can see in the map on page 111, which shows the discoveries of Columbus, with great blank areas of the New World marked "Unknown Land."

How thrilling such maps must have been to the people of the Renaissance! Printers and mapmakers were hard pressed to supply enough maps and atlases; and it was impossible for them to keep pace with the latest discoveries, as explorers pushed onward to unknown coasts and uncharted seas.

COMPASS AND DIVIDERS
from the title page of
The Mariners Mirrour
London, 1588

Ships and Navigation

HEN COLUMBUS SAILED FROM PALOS, IN Spain, in 1492, he set his course by the compass, the only dependable instrument of navigation that he had. Seamen had been using the compass since the Middle Ages. At first, the magnetized needle had been stuck through a straw and floated freely in a bowl of water. By the time of Columbus it was mounted on a pivot underneath a circular card, marked around the edge with the thirty-two points of the compass, and the needle and card were enclosed in a round box covered by transparent mica or glass.

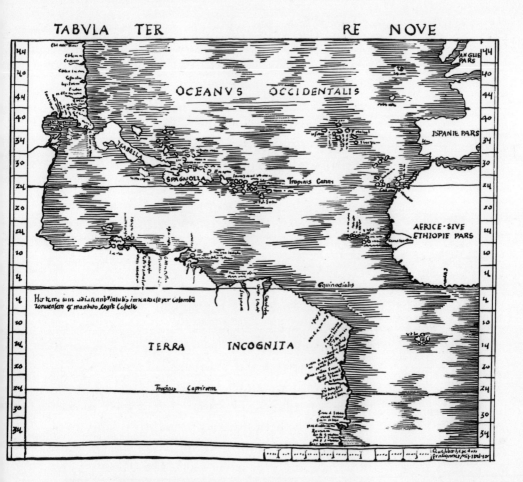

The earliest compasses surviving today were made for travelers on land. They were an ingenious combination of compass and pocket sundial for telling the time. The instrument opposite consists of two leaves of ivory, hinged together, with

MAP OF THE
NEW WORLD
from Ptolemy's
Geographia
Strassburg, 1513

111

a tiny compass mounted in the lower one under a circle of glass. When the thread, stretched between the leaves, is set by the compass to point north and south on a sunny day, the shadow it casts on the engraved table will tell the hour.

These little dials were made by craftsmen of Nuremberg, one of whom, in the late fifteenth century, published a road map called "The Road to Rome," designed to be used with a compass dial. The roads were marked off in dots to show mileage; and, by placing the dial with the needle pointing to the north end of the map, a traveler could easily find his way in strange country.

For sailors, at this time, there were detailed, hand-drawn charts of the Mediterranean and sailing directions for the coasts and harbors of northern Europe; but along unfamiliar shores, and in foggy weather, sailors had to feel their way by taking soundings. The lead line, which showed the depth of the water and brought up samples of sand or mud from the bottom, was one of the most important tools for navigation. This picture of an Elizabethan seaman with a lead line comes from the English edition of *The Mariner's Mirrour*, the first printed atlas of sea charts for sailors. The book was the work of a Dutch seaman, Lucas Wagenhaer, and it was such a success in England

USING THE LEAD LINE
from the title page of
The Mariners Mirrour
London, 1588

112

that all later books of charts were known there as "Waggoners."

It was comparatively easy for sailors to find their way along a charted coast. They could often take their bearings from landmarks. In the open sea there were no landmarks, and deep-water sailors, since ancient times, had looked to the sun and stars to guide them on their courses. Navigators like Columbus could steer by the compass, but they still had the problem of fixing their daily positions at sea, and marking them down precisely with a prick of the dividers on the great blank spaces of the Atlantic chart. Astronomers had long ago solved this problem of position by observing the sun and stars with special instruments, and the quadrant, shown at the right, was among the first of these instruments to be used by navigators.

With a quadrant the seaman could measure the height of the Pole Star and calculate from the result his latitude north of the Equator. He viewed the star through two little sights on the upper edge of the instrument and took a reading where the weighted plumb line cut across the scale of degrees. With the plumb line swinging to the roll of the ship, it was hard to read the instrument correctly at sea; and most navigators, including Columbus, made their observations ashore to fix

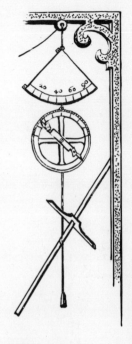

QUADRANT,
ASTROLABE
AND CROSS-STAFF
from the title page of
The Mariners Mirrour

the positions of newly discovered coasts and islands.

They could also find their latitude by using an astrolabe to measure the height of the sun at noon. The mariner's astrolabe was a simplified form of the elaborate and beautiful instruments used by astronomers. The astrolabe above belonged to the great French explorer, Samuel de Champlain, who used it for making observations in the Canadian wilderness. The instrument was found in the backwoods of Ontario in 1867, more than two centuries after Champlain had lost it there. It consists of a

ORIZONTE

heavy brass ring engraved with a scale of degrees around the upper half and with a pointer, or alidade, fastened in the center and fitted with two upright sights. The mariner's astrolabe was probably invented in Spain about 1530, and in one of the earliest handbooks for seamen, *The Art of Navigation* by Pedro de Medina, we find this picture of an astrolabe in use. The navigator holds the instrument hanging from his left hand and moves the alidade until the sun shines directly through the two sights. Then he reads off the number of degrees where the pointer crosses the scale.

OBSERVING THE
ALTITUDE OF THE SUN
WITH AN ASTROLABE
*from the Art of Navigation
by Pedro de Medina
Valladolid, 1545*

115

The mariner's astrolabe was popular with navigators until the early seventeenth century. The cross-staff which replaced it was a cheaper instrument, easier to make and use. The scale of degrees was marked along the staff, and the crossbar was moved back and forth until the top end of it lined up with the sun or the Pole Star. Sailors were taught to hold the cross-staff like a crossbow, and they talked of "shooting" the sun or the Pole Star, as sailors still do today.

During the sixteenth century a number of books were published on the art of navigation, and instruments for navigators were made with precision and skill. Wooden instruments, such as the quadrant and cross-staff, were the work of men trained as carpenters, using hard woods — boxwood, beech, and pear — which could be engraved with great accuracy. Brass would also take fine engraving, and the brass workers who made mariners' astrolabes worked as delicately as goldsmiths to be sure the markings were exact.

Makers of nautical instruments often had their workshops close to the shipyards, where seagoing ships were built, and the docks from which they set sail. There were the long, narrow galleys of the

116

Mediterranean, with oars and triangular lateen sails; the little lateen-rigged caravels which sailed along the Atlantic coasts of Europe and Africa; and, above all, the proud three-masted carracks, ships for the open ocean. With their combination of square and lateen sails, the carracks were handier and more seaworthy than any other ships of their time, and their rounded hulls, high in prow and

SHIPS OF THE
16TH CENTURY
*from Medina's
Art of Navigation*

117

stern, were roomy enough to carry a large crew with ample cargo and supplies. It was in full-rigged ships like these that many of the explorers made their great voyages of discovery.

The first carracks were built about 1450, probably by shipwrights along the Atlantic coasts of Spain, Portugal, or Brittany, and the new design was soon copied in Italy and northern Europe.

118

The shipwrights of each country passed on the secrets of their craft from father to son, working out improvements in hull and rigging until they could build such vessels as the Elizabethan warship displayed on the title page of an English handbook of navigation.

How proud the shipwrights must have been as their ships set sail from the harbors of Spain and Portugal, England, France, and Holland, bound for the New World, the Far East, or the icy seas of the North. There would be cheering crowds on the wharf and the sound of music when the ships moved slowly from the shore and the breeze filled their sails. The *Santa Maria,* the *Golden Hind,* the *Half Moon*! The shipbuilders are forgotten, but the famous ships they built are remembered forever in the stirring tales of the explorers' voyages.

The artists and craftsmen of those days were explorers, too. They cast off old ideas and old ways of working and pressed forward to the new. As we look today at the beautiful work of Renaissance craftsmen, we can catch a breath of their spirit of adventure and a glimpse of the exciting time in which they lived — the Age of Exploration, when the world was widened far beyond the boldest dreams of the explorers.

119

SHIP *from Saxton's large map of England and Wales, 1583*

LIST OF MUSEUMS

THE BRITISH MUSEUM, LONDON
Illustrations on Pages 32 (upper left), 96 (top), 99 (top), 103 (top), 105

THE METROPOLITAN MUSEUM OF ART, NEW YORK
Illustrations on Pages 2 (frontispiece), 19, 20, 21 (top), 22, 23 (top), 24 (top), 26 (top left), 29 (bottom), 30 (top), 31 (lower right), 34, 35 (right), 36 (top), 37 (top), 38, 39 (top), 40 (top), 41, 42 (top), 43 (right), 44, 45, 46, 47 (top), 48, 49, 50, 51, 52, 53, 54, 59, 60 (left), 61 (right), 62, 63, 64, 66 (top), 67, 68, 69, 72, 73 (top), 74 (top), 75 (right), 77, 78 (top), 79 (top), 80, 82 (top), 86, 87, 88 (top), 89, 90, 93 (top right), 94, 108, 110 (left)

THE MUSEUM OF FINE ARTS, BOSTON
Illustrations on Pages 28 (left), 29 (top), 102 (top)

THE NEW YORK HISTORICAL SOCIETY, NEW YORK
Illustration on Page 114

THE VICTORIA AND ALBERT MUSEUM, LONDON
Illustrations on Pages 10, 25 (top), 26 (left and top right), 27 (top), 30 (left), 31 (top), 32 (lower left), 33 (right), 35 (top), 39 (right), 47 (right), 56, 57, 58 (top), 60 (top), 61 (top), 65, 70, 71, 73 (right), 75 (top), 76 (left), 78 (left), 79 (right), 81 (right), 82 (left), 83, 84, 85 (right), 95, 96 (left), 97, 98 (right)

THE YALE SCHOOL OF MUSIC, NEW HAVEN
The viola da gamba on Page 91 (from the Morris Steinert Collection), the bugle on Page 92 (from the Belle Skinner Collection of Old Musical Instruments on loan to Yale University)

THE YALE UNIVERSITY ART GALLERY, NEW HAVEN
Illustrations on Pages 55, 66 (left)

120